This

Read, Listen, & Wonder

book belongs to:

CANDLEWICK PRESS

For Martin Llewellyn
K. W.

For my Dad
M. B.

First U.S. paperback edition with CD 2009

The Library of Congress has cataloged the hardcover edition as follows:

Wallace, Karen.
Think of an eel / written by Karen Wallace ;
illustrated by Mike Bostock. —1st U.S. ed.
(Read and wonder)
Summary: Text and illustrations discuss the characteristics and life cycle of the eel.
ISBN 978-1-56402-180-9 (hardcover)
1. Eels — Juvenile literature. [1. Eels.]
I. Bostock, Mike, ill. II. Title. III. Series.
QL637.9.A5W35   1993
597'.51—dc20   92-53131

ISBN 978-0-7636-1522-2 (paperback)
ISBN 978-0-7636-3994-5 (paperback with CD)

10 9 8 7 6 5 4 3 2 1

Printed in China

This book was typeset in Garamond.
The illustrations were done in watercolor.

Candlewick Press
99 Dover Street
Somerville, Massachusetts 02144

visit us at www.candlewick.com

Think of an Eel

Karen Wallace

illustrated by

Mike Bostock

CANDLEWICK PRESS

Think of an eel.

He swims like a fish.

He slides like a snake.

There's a warm, weedy sea
to the south of Bermuda.
It's called the Sargasso.
No wind ever blows there,
no sailing ships sail there.
For thousands of years there
a secret lay hidden:
This salt, soupy sea
is where eels are born.
Deep down where it's blackest,
eel egg becomes eel.
He looks like a willow leaf,
clear as a crystal.

Baby eels are born in early spring.
A real one is only

about this big.

His fierce jutting mouth
has teeth like a saw blade.

He eats like a horse and
swims up through the water.

Young eels from the Sargasso travel either to Europe or to America — whichever *their parents did before them.*

Imagine this eel-leaf
and millions just like him
swimming on waves
across the wide sea.
Some are unlucky.
The sea gulls are waiting.
Beaks snap like scissors
through wriggling water.

Eel swims for three years
till he reaches the shore,

but the river's too cold, there's
still snow on the mountains.

Eels arrive in Europe around Christmastime. They wait offshore

So he waits in the water,
turns into an elver.

Now he looks like a shoelace
made out of glass.

until spring, and as they wait they turn into elvers.

When spring

warms the shoreline,

the smell of fresh water

excites the glass elver.

Into the river

he swims like a mad thing.

He wriggles up rapids,

climbs rocks

around waterfalls.

Riverbanks guide him.

Nothing will stop him.

Eels navigate by instinct.

They always seem to know where they are going.

Around a drowned oak stump,
through twisting green weeds,
a mud hole is hidden.

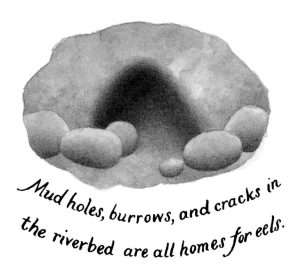

Mud holes, burrows, and cracks in the riverbed are all homes for eels.

Eel knows without thinking
it's what he's been seeking.
He slips through the ooze.
This hole is his home.

Think of an eel.
After years in the river
he's slit-eyed and slimy
and thick like a snake.
He gulps stickleback eggs,
eats shrimps and small fishes.

shrimp

Eels feed mostly at night.

If the river is empty
he swims from the mud hole,
slips through the grass
to steal snails from the pond.

pond snail

An eel can live out of water for two days or longer, if the ground is wet, breathing through its slimy skin.

One day eel stops eating.
His stomach is shrinking.
His long winding body
turns silver and black.
Eyes like black currants
bulge into headlights.
Now for the last time
eel slides from the mud hole.
His years in the river
are over forever.

Silver eels usually leave the river in September or October.

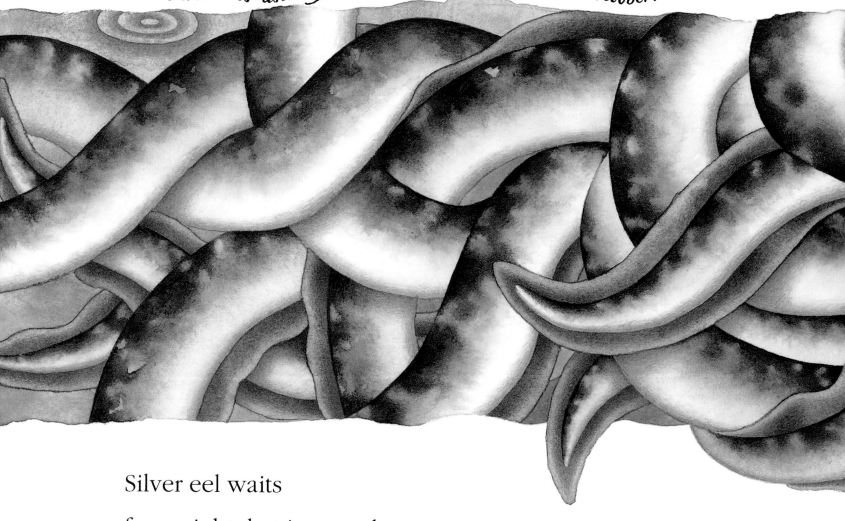

Silver eel waits

for a night that is moonless,

when the rain from the mountains

has flooded the stream.

While they're waiting for a dark night, they sometimes get tangled up in a ball.

Then he slips down the river, down to the seashore. The time has arrived for his long journey home.

For eighty days

silver eel swims through the ocean,

squirms like a secret

from seabird and sailor.

There are millions just like him,

deep down in the water,

swimming silently back

to the Sargasso Sea.

Eels have big eyes for seeing in the dark.

There's eel-tomb and eel-cradle
in the weedy Sargasso.
After eighty days swimming,
not eating, not sleeping,
eel's long, winding body
is worn-out and wasted.
He spills the new life
carried deep in his belly,
then sinks through the sea
like a used silver wrapper.

The male eel's sperm fertilizes the female's eggs in the water.

Deep down where it's blackest,
eel egg becomes eel.
He looks like a willow leaf,
clear as a crystal.
His fierce jutting mouth
has teeth like a saw blade.
He eats like a horse and
swims up through the water.

Imagine this eel-leaf
and millions just like him
swimming on waves
across the wide sea . . .

KAREN WALLACE has spent time fishing in the rivers of Ireland. She says she didn't see eels very often, but "when I did, I couldn't get over how extraordinary they were." Karen Wallace is the author of many picture books, including *Gentle Giant Octopus,* also illustrated by Mike Bostock.

MIKE BOSTOCK remembers catching eels as a child. "But reading the text was an education for me. I had no idea eels went through so many changes." Mike Bostock has illustrated several other picture books, including *Gentle Giant Octopus* by Karen Wallace.